CW01430632

A History of Sustainable Architecture:
Design Fundamentals

A History of Sustainable Architecture: Design Fundamentals

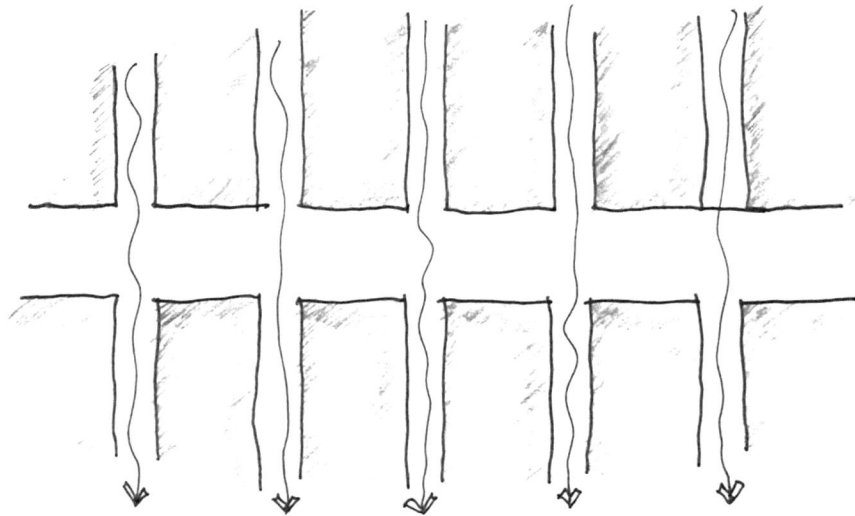

Suzanne Sowinski

Eco Press

First Printing, 2017

Printed in the United States

ISBN: 978-0-692-84179-2

Edited by Jennifer Yankopolus
Copyedited by Alison Jacques
Designed by Sandra Birchler

FSC
www.fsc.org

MIX
Paper from responsible sources
FSC® C103525

Eco Press
Philadelphia, PA 19102

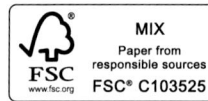

Captions:

Previous page: A street grid allows buildings, if property designed, to take advantage of passive ventilation

Next page: Warm air that builds up inside a structure during the day is transferred to the cool night sky, an ancient passive design technique

Publisher's Cataloging-In-Publication Data (Prepared by The Donohue Group, Inc.)

Names: Sowinski, Suzanne, author, illustrator.

Title: A history of sustainable architecture : design fundamentals / Suzanne Sowinski.

Description: Philadelphia, PA : Eco Press, 2017. | Includes bibliographical references and index.

Identifiers: ISBN 978-0-692-84179-2

Subjects: LCSH: Sustainable architecture--History. | Sustainable buildings--Design and construction--History.

Classification: LCC NA2542.36 .S69 2017 | DDC 720.47--dc23

To Richard Sullivan,
my husband and
best friend for
over 30 years

Contents

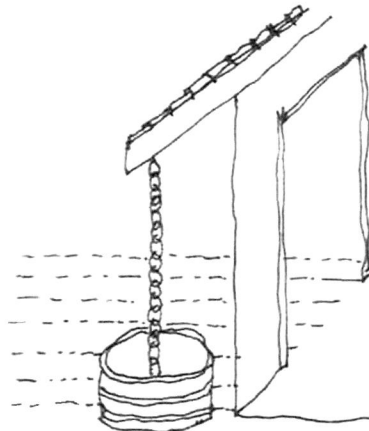

A rain chain
directs water
off the roof and
captures it for
reuse

Acknowledgments

This book has taken over ten years to contemplate, research, write, and revise. Several students volunteered along the way, helping with everything from compiling bibliographies to looking at different book designs and researching information, casting a wide net for what was necessary to tell this story. My children, Jonathan, Kristen, and Zachary, each offered and provided assistance at many stages of the process, living with me through the initial phase and riding the waves of the writing process. Nicole Fishstein, Amanda Holenstein, Brian Koval, Tony Policastro, Natalie Sutherland, and Kelly Wilson volunteered many hours of their time to help with the research in its early stages. Jill Cadorin, Lavinia Matulevich, Taryn Petrela, Shana Tracy, and Maureen Zeglen worked to develop the research that went into the initial vision of the book. I must thank the Boston Architecture College for giving me a grant to create the graduate course, Learning from Sustainable Design through History, for the school's Sustainable Design Institute—the endeavor that led to this book. I also thank my colleague David Foley, my professor and mentor, who reminded me of my love of the history of architecture. Finally, I am grateful to my husband for his regular reminders of the importance of this subject and for his understanding when the effort took time away from both our family and our firm.

Foreword

Many Americans are comfortably into their boomer years, and most of us were reared by parents and grandparents who lived through the Great Depression. Whether you were of immigrant families who came through Ellis Island during those years or were early settlers in the dusty wide spots on countless rural roads across the country, putting food on the table or shelter over your head took some inventiveness. You used what you could find and you used only what you needed because you didn't know what challenges tomorrow might bring.

This excellent exploration Suzanne Sowinski has provided reminds us that sustainability as applied to architecture is a way of thinking that would be familiar to our elders, and it's an ethic that stretches even further back in time. She notes many examples that date to primitive tribes, early Mediterranean civilizations, and the rise of the earliest cities: Indigenous people sited their nomadic habitats to use the sun's heat to best advantage; locally harvested materials—wood, mud, reeds, and stone—were fashioned into structures that could withstand the elements and keep families safe; and buildings of all kinds have used the natural terrain to regulate for comfort, adding features such as porches and porticos as the surroundings dictated.

But as we outgrew the resources of our local surroundings, as we became enamored with complex technology solutions for even the simplest problems, we became out of balance with our natural surroundings, and we lost sight of sustainable design as both a functional approach and an aesthetic promise that could nourish our souls even as it ensured our survival.

That's why in my role as founding chairman and CEO of the U.S. Green Building Council I've spent much of the past 25 years crisscrossing the globe advocating for sustainable buildings and a need to embrace the wisdom of our elders, whom I've often referred to as the original sustainability natives because they practiced sustainability as a matter of course.

How many of you remember the jar of buttons your mom kept in the linen closet, just in case? How many of you remember the jar of nails and screws of all shapes and sizes your dad kept with his tools, or the pieces of string he carefully put in a shoebox, even though many of them might be too short to be tied?

This appreciation of the smallest things, the traditional practices, underpins how we've made sustainable building practice relevant again. In the face of climate change, we've had to rethink how we heat and cool and light our buildings without doubling down on fossil fuel extraction that increases greenhouse gases and scars our landscape beyond repair. Throughout history, solving access to water was what allowed cities to take hold, and today the stakes are even higher as emerging economies are moving people further and further away from potable supplies. Material science has advanced our options on one side of the equation, but on the other, reuse and recycle suffers.

With catalysts like LEED, we've been able to remind this generation of architects and designers, construction professionals, and manufacturers that much wisdom exists in our history if we but pay heed. And the people and the planet we occupy will be better for it.

—Rick Fedrizzi
Chairman and CEO
International WELL Building Council

"The design of any building derives from considered responses to climate, technology, culture, and site. Architecture is born when, through intellectual deliberation, an inspired and appropriate balance between these four constituents is reached and a singular physical entity is created."

—David Lloyd Jones, Architect

Chapter One: The Historical Roots of Sustainability

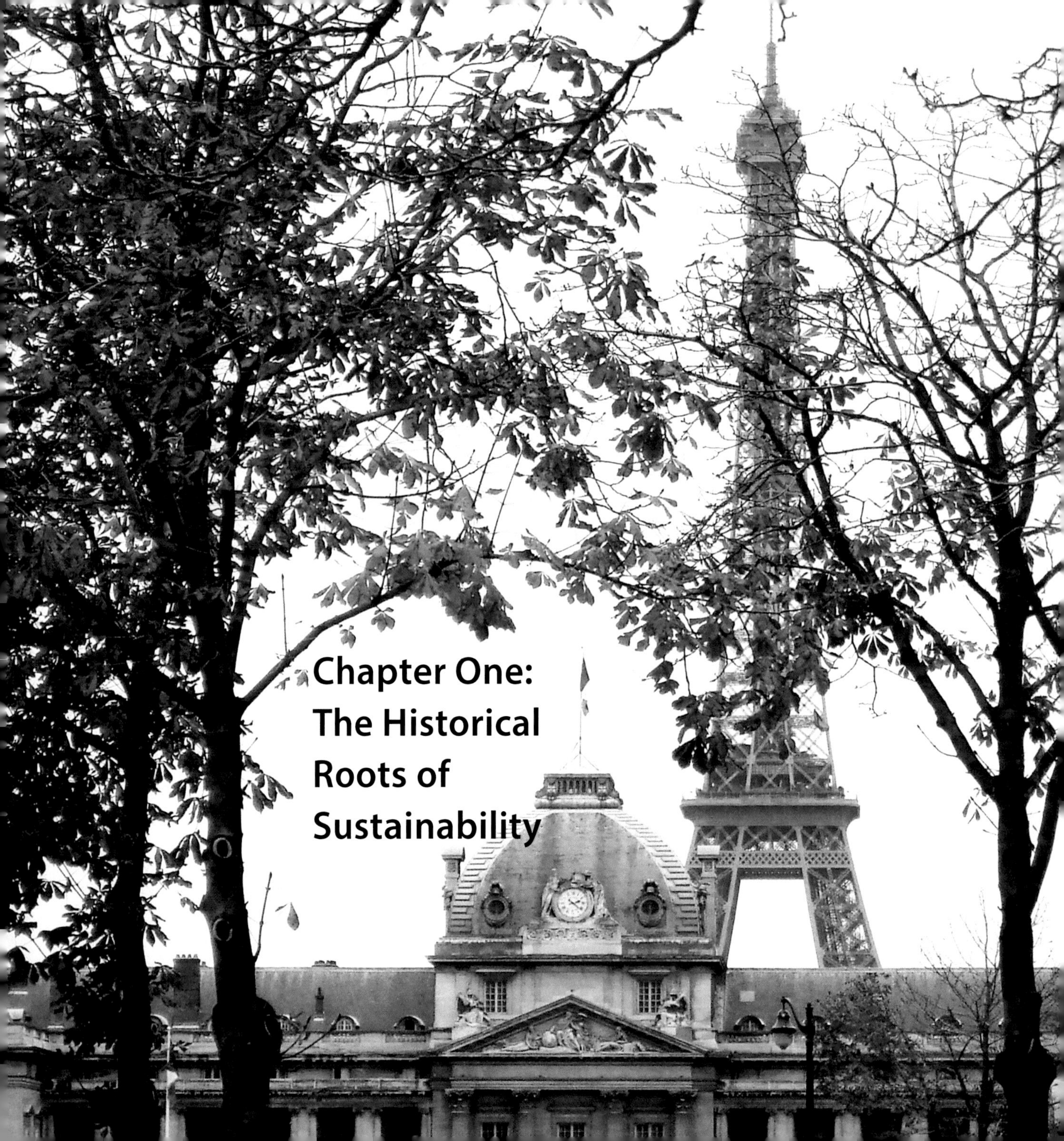

Sustainability in architecture is not, as is frequently believed, a 21st-century phenomena. Its roots extend to historical design and construction practices that incorporated nature, used efficient means for achieving comfort, provided for human needs, and sought minimally destructive ways to accomplish these end goals. Although the modern-day building industry has developed green building codes and green building rating systems, they are only tools. The intention behind these tools and the practices they encourage—building in harmony with nature—date back far into history.

The modern and the historic blend in London's skyline, England

The contemporary green movement is a real response to serious problems, not a fad. Climate change, overpopulation, and the growing scarcity of clean water and natural resources have made sustainability a global concern. The need to manage the planet's finite resources is critical. The building sector worldwide alone accounts for almost half of all energy used, which includes the power used for daily building operations, the manufacturing of building materials, building construction, and the demolition of buildings at the end of their useful life. Buildings also account for 70 percent of the daily water usage in the United States. As the world's population continues to increase, so too will the demand for new buildings, which in turn will consume more of the earth's raw materials. Therefore, architects, designers, engineers, builders, and building owners have a very important role to play in the responsible stewardship of our natural resources.

In ancient times, man used available means to build shelter from the elements

Many of the sustainability tools and approaches currently in use in the green architecture movement emanate from ancient design and building techniques that have been rediscovered and adapted to modern needs and conditions. Preindustrial cultures worked with, rather than ignored, the climate, available water sources, sun and wind patterns, and local resources in the design and construction of structures that provided shelter, enabled cohesive communities to be built, and produced enduring works of architecture reflective of their aspirations. Prior to the Industrial Revolution, according to Dean Hawkes, a professor of architectural design, "all architecture, whether noble or humble, was sustainable. From antiquity, buildings employed the properties of material and form to make appropriate adaptations to the relationships between their uses and the climates in which they were set. Their

Reconstruction of a teepee overlooking the Appalachian Mountains, Hardwick, New Jersey

design was based on sophisticated empirical understanding of quite complex physical processes and relationships."

Ancient cultures did, at times, have a negative impact on the environment. The ancient Romans and Greeks, for example, depleted their forests by overharvesting wood to use for heat, and quarrying stone still scarred the earth, even with the nonmechanical methods used by preindustrial cultures. However, since the Industrial Revolution, the scale and pace at which humanity has mistreated the natural world has grown exponentially.

Our landfills are filled with non-biodegradable materials, including used building products

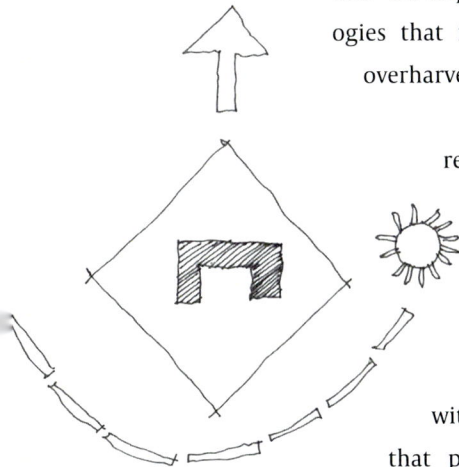

History offers us real lessons on how to respect the environment and a chance to revisit knowledge about how to build in a way that creates a healthy relationship with nature. By looking back to history, we can enhance our efforts to envision and develop sustainable architecture that is appropriate for the world we currently live in. We can learn from the creative solutions our ancestors developed that provided for their basic human needs—without technologies that fill landfills with nonbiodegradable plastics and batteries, without overharvesting natural resources, and without polluting the environment.

Humanity has coexisted with nature and managed the planet's resources since prehistoric times. "The history of green architecture is basically the history of mankind," writes Osman Attmann, the author of *Green Architecture: Advanced Technologies and Materials.* "The relationships among man, environment, and ecology were established the day the first humans (hominids) appeared on the scene." Today, combining ancient design and construction methods with modern materials and engineering techniques can create architecture that preserves our affluent lifestyle without impoverishing our planet.

Orienting a building to the patterns of the sun offers many sustainable benefits

Ancient buildings
in harmony
with nature,
a view from
Boboli Gardens,
Florence, Italy

Chapter Two:
Sticks and Stones

Well before recorded history, humans built structures with materials they could harvest locally, such as wood, mud, reeds, and stone, using the tools available to them. To be turned into something usable, these raw materials often had to be processed in some way. Mud was pressed into bricks. Tree branches were woven into walls, (wattle and daub) similar to weaving a basket. Wood and stone were shaped into functional forms. These materials differed in their durability as well. Reeds, papyrus, and palm branches were commonly used for roofs, walls, and flooring, but would have to be replaced frequently because of how easily they break down. Conversely, structures built with stone, kiln-dried bricks, and hardwood could better withstand damage from water, wind, and sun. The processes of making wood, stone, and metal into building materials have effects on the environment. Although a mud-brick can be made more durable by firing it in a kiln, that process requires the burning of wood, coal, or another fuel source, which emits carbon dioxide and methane into the atmosphere. Mining these resources can also cause deforestation, leave unsightly wounds in the earth, and damage the surrounding ecosystem. And in the case of metal, the process of turning the raw material into a final product is energy intensive and creates pollutants.

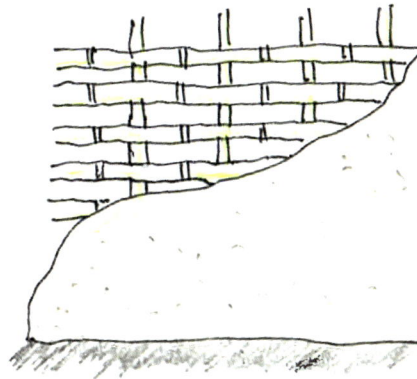

Wattle and daub construction

Although building products developed during and after the Industrial Revolution have broadened the materials and systems options available, designers and specifiers have given little attention to the amount of energy and resources that are consumed by manufacturing these new materials. As advancements in transportation have expanded, it has also become easier and cheaper to transport building products all over the world, which increases their carbon footprint (the amount of carbon dioxide released into the air). For building products to be sustainable, there must be a balance between their impact on the environment and their durability. The goal should be to design buildings using materials with a smaller overall carbon footprint by reducing the amount of raw materials used to make new building materials, using reclaimed building materials and manufacturing by-products to make new materials, and selecting durable building materials that are manufactured locally.

Where once building materials were harvested locally, today cargo ships transport them worldwide

One of the oldest building materials is the earth's surface, alternately referred to as mud, clay, silt, and soil, depending on its composition. Bricks made with mud were widely used to construct buildings during ancient times, especially in places where trees and stones were scarce. The technique used to make mud-bricks has changed very little since 8000 BC when the mud-brick walls and buildings of the city of Jericho, one of the oldest inhabited cities in the Western world, were constructed. All the materials were harvested and processed from the building site, and the mud was mixed with water and straw or another type of binder, placed in a mold, and

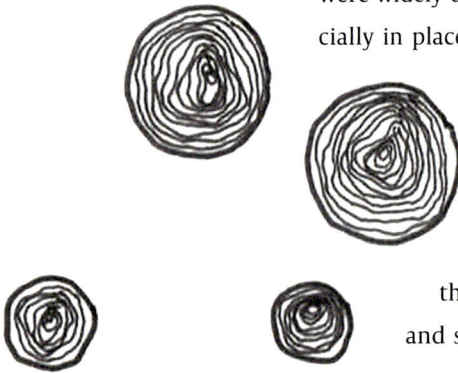

Harvested wood for construction

10

dried in the sun. Structures made with sun-dried mud-bricks, also known as adobe bricks, are more susceptible to deterioration than kiln-dried bricks. Because the mud-bricks are dried in the sun, rather than fired in a kiln, changes in temperature and moisture will shrink and swell them, causing brick walls to shift and potentially compromising their structural integrity. Nevertheless, in places where the climate is conducive to using sun-dried mud-bricks, ancient structures built with this material are still standing, including parts of the Great Wall of China (built between 2600 and 1900 BC) and portions of the Alhambra in Granada, Spain (AD 1238–1358).

Sun-dried mud-bricks are an economical and sustainable material that continues to be used today, especially in places with a tradition of mud-brick construction, such as North Africa, Peru, Central America, the Middle East, and China. In most instances,

Portions of the Great Wall of China date as far back as 2600 BC

especially in the United States, the raw materials are not usually harvested from the building site; instead, the bricks are commercially manufactured off-site. Modern-day mud-brick construction also adds steel rods to the walls and foundation for reinforcement. Compared to structures made with wood, mud-brick walls are thicker, which increases their thermal mass. Materials with a higher thermal mass absorb and store more heat, keeping the interior at a more consistent temperature and requiring less supplemental heating and cooling. Sun-dried mud-bricks are best suited for hot and dry climates, where they are less susceptible to deterioration. Using adequate roof overhangs that will shed water away from the building also helps extend the life of mud-brick structures.

Baking a mud-brick in a kiln makes it stronger, more durable, and less susceptible to degradation from moisture. A kiln-dried brick—what we generally call a brick—has been a popular material for thousands of years. Even though the expected life of a brick building is 100 years, many examples of ancient brick buildings still survive, such as parts of the Great Wall of China and Roman aqueducts (the oldest dating back to 312 BC). Because of variations in the soil around the world, ancient bricks differed in color depending on the region in which they were produced. Bricks are a common building material today, but rather than being structural, they often function as an exterior weather barrier (or cladding) or a decorative layer atop the underlying structure. Bricks are considered sustainable because of their durability, strength, high recycled content, and ability to be recycled

An ancient Roman aqueduct

into new bricks, but the manufacturing process does require a fuel source.

Another form of kiln-dried clay is terra-cotta, which is used for nonstructural components like drainpipes, pottery, statues, and decorative architectural features. The use of terra-cotta dates back to 10,000 BC in China and the Near East. Beginning around 700 BC, the ancient Greeks perfected the mass production of terra-cotta roof tiles using molds, and terra-cotta tiles replaced dried reeds and palms, which decayed quickly and were prone to fire. Terra-cotta can be easily pressed into different shapes, making it useful for producing ornamental details and functional elements. For example, the bottom edges of a Greek roof used terra-cotta tiles that were bent upward, acting as a gutter that channeled rainwater into animal-shaped heads made from terra-cotta placed at the corners of the building. When it rained, water flowed from their mouths, which acted as a drip edge, protecting the building from water damage. The Tower of the Winds, built around 50 BC in Athens, was adorned with lion heads that funneled water off the roof through the lions' mouths. Gutters, roof overhangs, and a steep roof pitch all prevent water from seeping into the foundation and causing deterioration to a building's

The Tower of the Winds, Athens, Greece

Unglazed terra-cotta roof tiles, Siena, Italy

13

walls, roof, and foundation. Using a durable material like terra-cotta tiles for the roof and its components extends the life of a building and lowers maintenance costs.

Because of its efficient production process, ability to withstand freezing temperatures, ability to be manufactured in repetitive stylistic designs, and fire-proofing quality, terra-cotta became a popular building product in the United States during the 1800s. Terra-cotta is easy to maintain and can be manufactured locally. Currently in the United States, architectural terra-cotta is used primarily when restoring buildings that already contain terra-cotta. As a roofing material, terra-cotta tiles are more expensive and heavier than other roofing materials, such as metal and asphalt shingles, and require the roof to be reinforced to support the added weight. The life-span of a terra-cotta roof is at least 100 years, compared to 30 years for asphalt shingles. Along with its many sustainable attributes, terra-cotta can be recycled at the end of its life and used to make new terra-cotta. New terra-cotta contains both postconsumer content (waste by consumers) and preconsumer content (waste from the manufacturing process). Using recycled content is an important practice when manufacturing new materials; it diverts waste that would otherwise end up in a landfill and reduces the amount of virgin resources that are extracted from the earth.

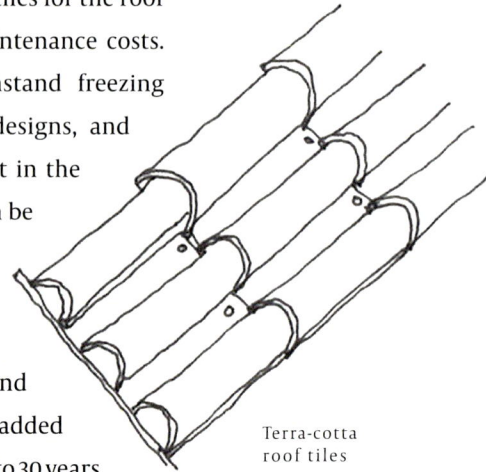

Terra-cotta
roof tiles

In areas where it was readily available, wood has long been used to construct buildings, foundations, walls, columns, beams, and interior finishes and furniture. The knowledge and skill required to build with wood advanced during the Neolithic period. During the medieval period in Europe, wood framing was a common technique to build barns for monasteries in which heavy-timber (large sawn timber) posts and beams were

Traditional
Scandinavian heavy
timber construction

used to support the structure. Similar to the nave and center aisle layout found in Early Christian cathedrals, these barns were often constructed with a three-part framing system, such as the structures at the St. Gall monastery in Switzerland (640–720 AD). This approach allowed the barns to be easily expanded, rather than having to demolish them and construct new ones in their place. Historically, hand tools were used to cut the trees down and shape the wood into boards and columns. Later, sawmills powered by water transformed the raw wood into lumber.

The use of heavy-timber framing is not as common today because of the time it takes for hardwood trees to grow to a size sufficient for the large cross section found in large sawn lumber. Additionally, the knowledge required to build with this system is now a specialized skill. Instead, laminated wood beams, which are manufactured by gluing together layers of wood harvested from smaller trees, are used for longer spans. In the United States, dimensional lumber (two-by-fours and two-by-sixes), which is used for framing houses and commercial buildings, boardwalks, and decks, is commonly made from

Dimensional lumber framing

southern pine trees because of their shorter growing period. To improve its durability, dimensional lumber is dried to a maximum moisture content of 19 percent, which minimizes shrinkage. Hardwoods like oak and softwoods like pine are more durable than fast-growing plants like reeds, palms, and bamboo, but wood forests should be properly managed. Regulating the cutting and planting of trees is important to ensure that these resources will not be quickly depleted and that the ecosystem of the forests will remain intact.

A wall constructed
with bamboo

Bamboo is also a popular material because of its quick growth and strength. It is stronger than steel in both tensile strength (the ability to resist being pulled apart lengthwise along its grain) and compression strength (the ability to be crushed against its grain); however, its strength will be compromised if it is not waterproofed. There are countless ways to use bamboo in buildings. It can be made into corrugated sheets as an alternative to a metal roof or veneer sheets for use in doors, interior panels, furniture, flooring, and structural members. Unlike hardwood and softwood forests, which must be actively managed to avoid deforestation, bamboo regenerates itself; the root system on harvested plants will start to regrow, eliminating the need to replant.

Stone is one of the most naturally durable and strong materials. It is valued for the variety in color, texture, and veining patterns it offers, all of which vary depending on the land from which it is quarried. Quarrying stone has a negative effect, leaving an open void in the earth. Historically, hand tools were used to extract and shape stone; today, heavy machinery is used, which increases the environmental impact of quarrying on the surrounding area. Buildings constructed with stone have lasted centuries, providing us with many inspiring architectural examples around the world. Some of the most well-

Quarried
stone
columns

known stone structures are the Egyptian pyramids and tombs for pharaohs that were built over the course of many dynasties (2630–1640 BC) using limestone, granite, alabaster, and basalt. To extend the durability of these monuments, small holes—called weep holes—were integrated into the walls to allow any water that accumulated inside to drain. Water trapped inside a stone structure can damage its integrity. The Great Wall of China, which in places was constructed of stone, also incorporated weep holes as well as drain spouts and channels to drain trapped water.

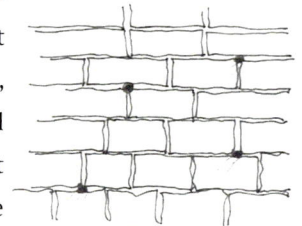
Weep holes in
a brick wall

16

In buildings today, stone is typically used in a nonstructural way as exterior decorative cladding over a structural frame composed of metal or concrete block. Less stone is needed for cladding than for load-bearing stone walls. Weep holes are still commonly used in stone construction, whether or not the stone is structural, to prevent moisture from being trapped in the hollow space between the exterior cladding and the interior wall. Control joints are also used, allowing stone walls to expand and contract with temperature fluctuations or building movement. Using weep holes and similar techniques to extend a building's life-span conserves the natural resources that would be consumed to construct a new building in its place.

Even though concrete had been in use since before the Roman era, the ancient Romans perfected its use as a building material. As the Roman Empire expanded, so did the demand for buildings, and concrete construction provided an economical and practical solution. The Romans had an abundance of volcanic soil, which, when mixed with lime, produced a concrete of unprecedented strength and malleability. The

The construction techniques developed by the Romans allowed many structures to survive into the 21st century, The Forum, Rome, Italy

ubiquity of these raw materials and the fact that concrete could be made by unskilled laborers helped spread concrete construction across the empire, producing a uniformity in the architecture. Concrete was primarily used for the underlying structure and was then covered with marble, brick, or other stone for decorative effect. The structural integrity and the pliability of concrete aided the advancement of structural systems like arches, vaults, and domes, reducing the need for vertical supports and creating the possibility of larger uninterrupted interior spaces. The Coliseum (AD 70), the Baths of Caracalla (AD 211–217), a number of Roman aqueducts, and many other ancient Roman buildings that still stand were made with concrete and faced with stone or bricks. The Pantheon, built by Emperor Hadrian and completed in AD 125, is the largest unreinforced dome ever built out of concrete. The dome acts as a calendar: the beam of sunlight shining through the opening in the center of the dome illuminates different parts of the interior as the seasons change.

The Coliseum, Rome, Italy

Because it is so durable and economical, concrete construction is quite common today. Manufacturing concrete involves extracting the raw materials (sand, lime, and crushed stone) and combining them with water. In the past 20 years, it has become popular to use coal ash, a by-product

The Hoover Dam, Arizona and Nevada

from coal-fueled power plants that would normally end up in a landfill, as the binder in concrete. Many structural materials and buildings—such as the Hoover Dam, built in 1939 in Nevada and Arizona—contain some amount of fly ash, also known as coal ash. The concrete used in the foundation, core, supporting columns, and floor slabs of the Freedom Tower in New York City (2006-2012) also contains fly ash. Fly ash has other uses in the construction world, from carpet backing to the decking used to grow plants on a green roof.

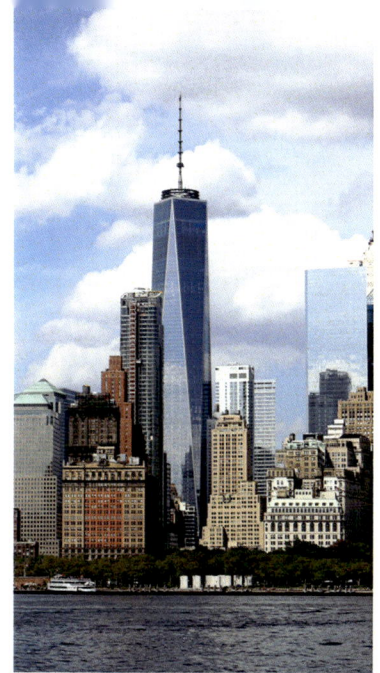

The Freedom Tower, New York, New York

The Industrial Revolution created many new building technologies and processes that changed the face of architecture and construction, particularly metal. The Chinese first produced cast iron around the 6th century BC, but it was not until the late 1700s that the technology was developed to mass produce it, allowing it to be manufactured cheaply and in sufficient quantities to be used on a large scale. Cast iron has fewer structural limitations than the conventional building materials that were in use at the beginning of the Industrial Revolution, such as heavy timber and stone. It was first used to build bridges. Compared with bridges made with stone or brick, cast iron bridges were lighter, had longer spans, and required fewer and smaller vertical supports, which displaced less water and reduced the likelihood of flooding. Cast iron was first used architecturally for the structural framing in factories and then became the norm in the many large-scale industrial and commercial projects built in Europe and the United States during the Industrial Revolution. By the late 19th century, cast iron was replaced by steel.

Cast iron construction, Eiffel Tower, Paris, France

19

When steel is used for a building's underlying structure, the thickness of the columns and the exterior walls can be reduced, allowing more light to enter the interior spaces and giving the building a lighter appearance. Although steel is very durable, one of the drawbacks of using metal is that when it is used in large buildings and certain building types, it needs to be fireproofed. Even though metal is incombustible, its strength is jeopardized when exposed to fire. Metal is a key component in tall buildings. Steel construction allows buildings of unprecedented heights with less of a footprint, leaving open space for parks or additional real estate. On the other hand, taller buildings can cast shadows on neighboring properties and streets, blocking sunlight for those occupants. Extracting metal from iron ore is a resource-intensive process.

Modern steel skyscrapers, Shanghai, China

If not properly done, it can cause air, water, and soil pollution, and the hazardous waste material it generates needs to be disposed of correctly. The mining process also poses various environmental risks, such as groundwater contamination and pollution from mining equipment.

Besides using durable materials that extend a building's life span, reusing building materials is another way to limit consumption of natural resources. A number of ancient cultures reused building materials. Wood, abundant in ancient China, was an integral part of its architecture, both decoratively and structurally. During the Han dynasty (206–220 BC), the Chinese

Decorative and structural wood brackets, Asia

perfected the technique of notching wood to connect columns and beams, called mortise-and-tenon, that later spread to Korea and Japan. Since this joining technique did not use nails or screw fasteners, the wood could be disassembled and reused without any holes or damage. In Japan it was common practice to remove wood architectural members from collapsed buildings. This salvaged material was often used to rebuild damaged or destroyed buildings, as was done for the Temple at Honmonji in Tokyo, originally erected in 1608. During the reign of Sultan Saladin (1174–1193) in Egypt, stone from the Giza pyramids was stripped and used in the construction of the Citadel in Cairo. Later, after an earthquake in 1356, stone from the Giza pyramids was used to rebuild Cairo's mosques and fortresses.

Salvaging components from a building that is abandoned or about to be demolished keeps waste out of landfills, while reusing reclaimed materials in new buildings conserves energy and water resources that would otherwise be expended to produce new materials. However, some energy is needed for the repurposing, and there are limits to how salvaged materials can be repurposed. For instance, it is easier to make stone into aggregate than to reuse it in its original state. Terra-cotta and brick can be reused in the manufacturing of new terra-cotta and brick, and concrete can be crushed and used as aggregate in new concrete. Recycling metal consumes less energy than manufacturing new metal, making it one of the more commonly recycled materials today. Some reclaimed materials can be reused with minimal reprocessing; for example, wood from old barns can be reused for flooring and antique bricks and sidewalk pavers can be reused in new walkways.

Mortise-and-tenon construction

The Great Pyramid of Giza

A floor made with reclaimed wood from a horse stable, Elixr Café, Philadelphia, Pennsylvania

Judging how sustainable a building product is can be a complicated task for architects and designers. It is challenging to calculate a product's environmental impacts, with such considerations as where and how the raw materials were harvested, the amount of pollution the harvesting and manufacturing generated, and the total number of miles that a product and its components traveled. The stated environmental benefits of a product can be misleading as well. Even if the materials are harvested from a managed forest, for example, it might take a huge amount of energy to turn them into a building product. Therefore, the product or system selection process must be rigorous to avoid being misled about its environmental impacts via promises made by manufacturers—a phenomenon known as greenwashing.

Quarrying not only scars the earth but damages the ecosystem

The time it takes to construct a building (one to five years on average) is relatively short compared with a commercial building's useful life (30 years or more). Therefore, using more durable materials—even if they are more expensive—will save money over the long term; they will have to be replaced less frequently, which will also slow the extraction of raw materials. To create truly sustainable buildings, we should minimize the amount of raw resources we consume, use less energy to make and transport building products, and minimize the amount of building materials added to our landfills and ocean floors. Using recycled building products or by-products of manufacturing processes should be made a priority before raw materials are extracted to make new products. We must achieve a balance between our need for safe, comfortable, functional buildings and what we take from the earth to build and renovate those structures.

Chapter Three:
Passive Design

T he construction, operation, and demolition of buildings contribute to climate change. In particular, the fossil fuels used to heat, cool, ventilate, and illuminate buildings release harmful carbon dioxide into the atmosphere. From their construction to their daily operation, buildings generate 30 percent of annual greenhouse gases globally and are responsible for 40 percent of worldwide energy usage. Before there were mechanical heating and cooling systems and electric lights, people kept their buildings comfortable by incorporating natural light and ventilation as well as regional climate patterns into the architecture—an approach that today we call passive design. In the last few decades, there has been a growing awareness in the design community that integrating these ancient practices into modern structures can reduce the amount of fossil fuels buildings consume while still

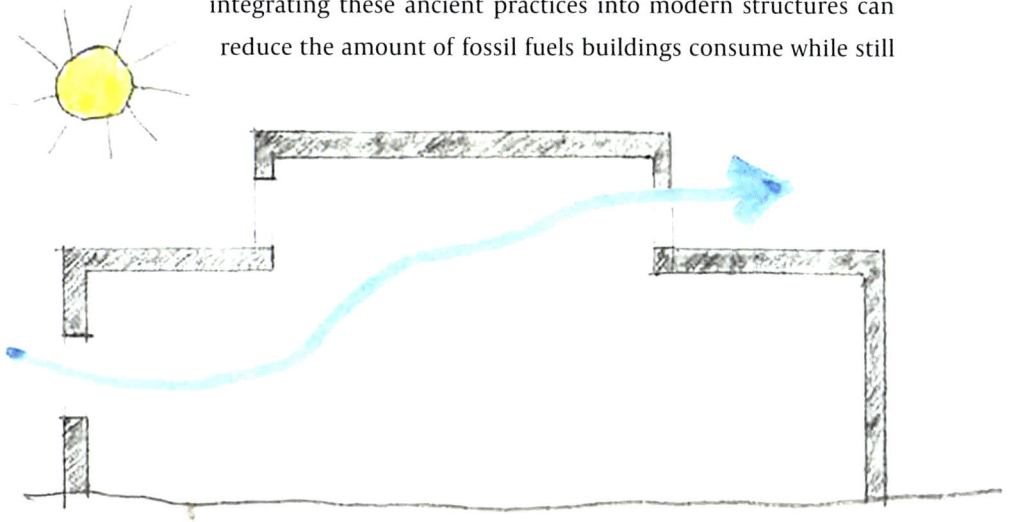

Incorporating passive
ventilation helps cool
buildings naturally

creating pleasant, functional spaces. In addition, passive design techniques will increase a building's energy efficiency and ultimately reduce global warming.

Central heating, air conditioning, and artificial illumination provide improved efficiency, better indoor air quality, and greater convenience. These inventions, and others, were made possible as a result of the Industrial Revolution—particularly, advances in power technology, like the steam engine, and the development of the modern energy industry. Before the Industrial Revolution, energy was generated primarily

Climate change is causing glaciers to melt, Svalbard Islands, Norway

by burning trees, other plant material, and dung; capturing the force of water; or harnessing the power of the wind and animals, in addition to using a small amount of petroleum and coal. Beginning in the early 1900s, coal, petroleum, and natural gas became the primary energy sources in developed countries. As a result of these advances, many of the passive design techniques that had been in use for much of recorded history were gradually abandoned in favor of modern mechanical systems, causing

The steam engine was a key component of the Industrial Revolution

a greater reliance on fossil fuels. We now understand that using petroleum and coal harms the environment.

Recently, architecture has begun to refocus on building in harmony with local conditions and using design strategies that conserve energy. Passive design techniques reduce our dependence on coal, oil, and other nonrenewable fuels and do not cause damage to air and water, which are, of course, essential to the survival of humans, animals, and plant life. The purpose of passive design is not to eliminate central heating, air-conditioning systems, or artificial light, but rather to design in a smarter way that uses nature to augment mechanical systems, creating comfortable spaces that reduce our consumption of natural resources.

The Industrial Revolution supplanted non-mechanical means at the cost of pollution and other harms to the environment

27

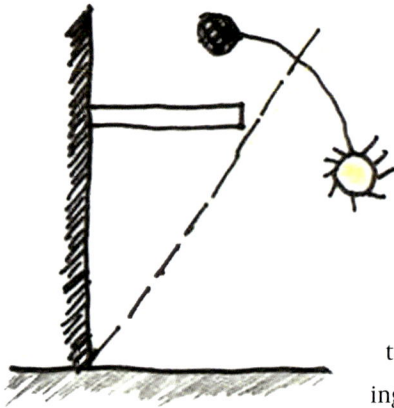

An overhang can be used to shade the building from the heat of the sun

Designing buildings to take advantage of the natural terrain, the presence of bodies of water, the amount of precipitation, the path of the sun throughout the seasons, and wind patterns can lower energy usage if such data is understood and used by designers. History provides us with many examples of building techniques that enhance people's comfort inside buildings in a way that does not deplete nonrenewable energy sources. One approach for channeling air though a building is a malkaf, or wind catcher—part of the vocabulary of ancient Egyptian architecture, dating back to 1300 BC. A wind catcher is

An example of a wind catcher, Iran

Modern geothermal loops extract heat from the ground and pump it into the building

placed on or above the roof to catch the wind and funnel it through the building, helping to cool the interior. Another example of natural ventilation dates from the 16th century in Vicenza, Italy, where natural caves, or covoli, were used as a cooling system. Six villas were built into the nearby hills and connected to the caves through vertical shafts. The wind produced in the caves by natural convection piped cool air into the villas; this natural air conditioning was similar to modern-day geothermal cooling systems.

Using outside air to ventilate buildings was common until the development and widespread use of central heating and cooling systems, when buildings began to be sealed off from the outside with inoperable windows. Closing off buildings from the outside seemed like a logical and efficient way to regulate the interior environment. Mechanical systems can control the climate inside a building regardless of the conditions outside, and insulating the building from the fluctuating outside air allows the system to function more efficiently. From a sustainability standpoint, relying solely on artificial heating, cooling, ventilation, and lighting systems is not environmentally responsible, nor is it cost effective, especially as energy demands

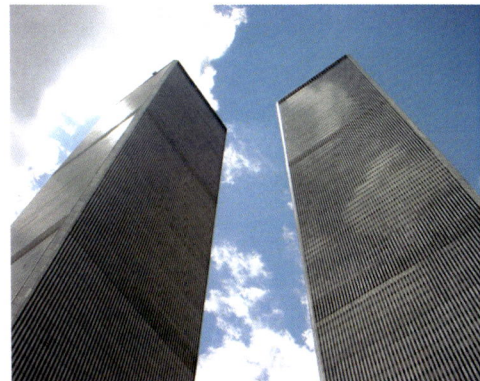

The World Trade Center towers, like all modern skyscrapers, were sealed off from the outside, New York, New York

29

Operable windows
enable cross ventilation,
a natural way to cool a
building

rise along with the world's population. Additionally, the notion that a homogeneous level of comfort can be achieved across a 5,000-square-foot (or larger) floor with a mechanical system is erroneous. Because sun and wind conditions vary from one side of a building to another, the indoor climate will fluctuate in different parts of the building despite its air-conditioning and heating system.

Ancient techniques such as using a wind catcher to capture the prevailing winds can be used to naturally ventilate buildings today. Something as simple as placing operable windows across from one another to allow cross ventilation is also effective. The skill is in designing the interior in a way that works in conjunction with seasonal wind patterns. Designers should analyze the natural airflow at the building site to guide the building's orientation, site design, floor plan, and form to maximize natural ventilation.

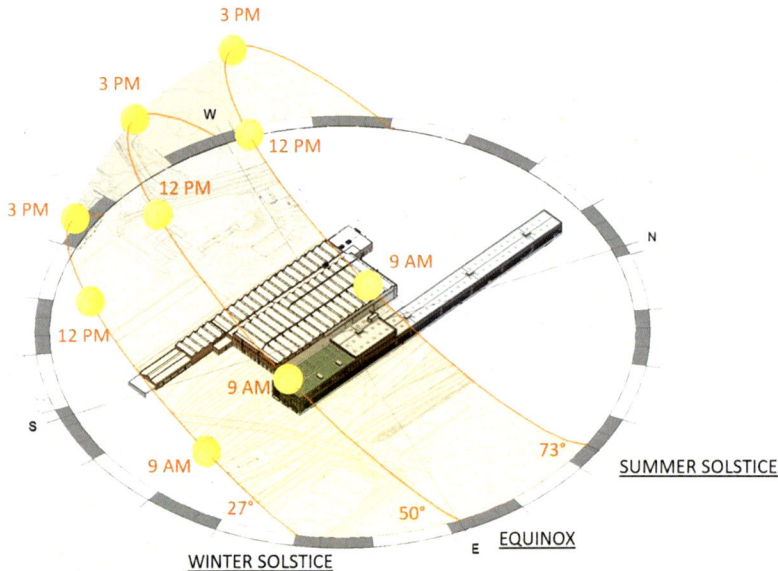

A building site plan
showing how the
sun patterns change
throughout the year,
Harmon Yards,
Harmon, New York

The composition of a building's roof is another passive design concept that can have an effect on the interior temperature. The Sumerians, for example, covered their mud dwellings with light-colored materials like palm trunks and reeds, which reduced the amount of the sun's heat that was transferred inside. Light-colored roofs absorb less heat than dark-colored roofs. A light-colored roof also reflects less heat back into the atmosphere, which can reduce the heat-island effect. The heat-island effect occurs in densely populated areas, which experience higher temperatures because of the prevalence of hard, dark surfaces—such as streets and buildings—that absorb the sun's heat and radiate it into the surrounding environment. A green roof can also lower the heat-island effect. As plants on a green roof absorb water

Many ancient cultures in the Mediterranean used light-colored roofs to keep the interiors cool, Marrakech, Morocco

A green roof naturally insulates a building and helps to cool the surrounding streets, Colts Intermodal Transit Center, Scranton, Pennsylvania

31

and release it back into the atmosphere through the process of transpiration, the temperature around the roof is reduced. Roofing material is an important consideration not only for reducing reliance on artificial cooling systems but also because decreasing the outside air temperature minimizes smog and the formation of greenhouse gases, slowing the earth's warming.

Orienting a building or group of buildings to take advantage of the path of the sun and the prevailing breezes is a straightforward and economical way of reducing energy consumption and a building's carbon footprint. The ancient Greeks planned their cities to allow citizens the right to access the warm winter sun and shade during the hot summer months. They achieved this in part by taking advantage of the mountainous topography, terracing the houses down the hillside. Priene, on the coast of Anatolia, is one of the first examples of sophisticated town planning in ancient Greece. Its grid of streets was laid out in conjunction with the natural contours of the land, and its houses were built along the south-facing mountain slope, offering each a north-facing courtyard in which occupants were shaded from the heat.

Today, when planning a community or siting an individual building, passive design principles can easily be incorporated—for example, orienting a building in an east–west direction to capture the heat and light of the sun or blocking that heat during the summer through the use of overhangs on the south, east, and west sides. Vegetation can also reduce heating and cooling costs; a mass of trees can act as a windbreak in the winter, reducing heating requirements, and can shade the building in the summer, reducing cooling requirements.

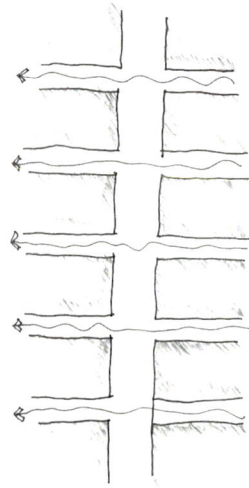

Properly orienting the street grid facilitates wind flow, which can naturally ventilate the buildings

Courtyards provide many passive benefits, Santa Maria del Carmine, Florence, Italy

A courtyard is not only a pleasant private outdoor space that is open to the sky but also a passive design solution. In China, courtyards date back to the 11th century BC and were designed in many different configurations depending on the climate and topography. Those found in the cold, dry northern parts of China were generally large and open, while in the hot, humid south they were smaller and more compact to restrict the amount of sun that could penetrate.

Courtyard at the Mont Saint-Michel Abbey, Normandy, France

Courtyards can provide many passive benefits today if they are oriented to the local climate and the path of the sun. The natural light that enters a courtyard can help illuminate the building's interior if windows are properly incorporated into the design. A courtyard can also help heat or cool a building. In warmer months, overhangs in the courtyard can block the sunlight, limiting unwanted heat buildup inside. Because the sun is lower in the winter sky, the overhangs should be designed to allow the sun and its warmth to reach the interior during the colder months. A courtyard in conjunction with properly placed and sized windows can funnel wind through a building to lower the temperature, or the height of its walls can be designed to block the wind. Today, courtyards are commonly used in public buildings like schools, office complexes, and multifamily housing developments, but less so in single-family homes because of limited space and people's desire for a backyard.

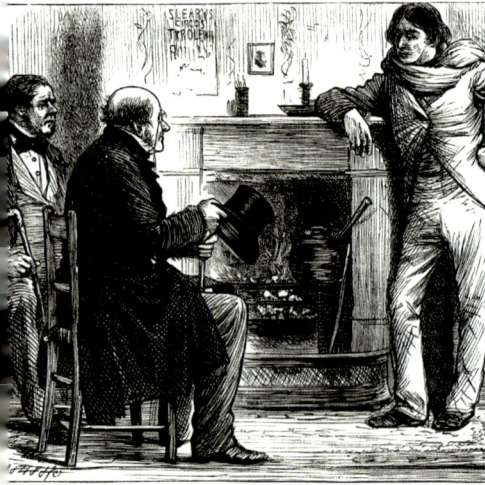

Fireplaces were a common heat source prior to the invention and widespread use of mechanical heating systems

Even though preindustrial cultures did not have central heating, they were able to keep their buildings comfortable by using passive design techniques in conjunction with burning wood or other plant material, dung, or coal. They also used passive lighting techniques in combination with burning wood and oil for illumination. One such passive heating and lighting technique is the clerestory window, located above eye level near the ceiling. The Romans used clerestory windows to heat and illuminate

The Romans used a hypocaust, a central heating system, to heat the water in the public baths, ancient city of Kourian, Cyprus

34

Glass-vaulted
ceilings were often
used to illuminate
shopping arcades,
a new building
type in the second
half of the 19th
century, Galleria
Vittorio Emanuele,
Milan, Italy

their buildings, especially their public baths; they also heated the baths with an under-floor heating system, a hypocaust, which required a large amount of fire-wood. By incorporating clerestory windows into the south-facing facade, they were able to capture the sun's heat and light, and by covering the openings with glass or mica, they protected bathers from rain and snow and trapped the heat inside.

If designed correctly, clerestory windows are an efficient way to save energy. They can decrease the need for artificial light, and, if the windows are operable, they can help cool a space by letting hot air escape and cool breezes pass through. But if a building is not oriented to take advantage of the sun and wind patterns, having clerestory windows can hinder the comfort level inside, making it too cold or too warm. Clerestory windows can also help regulate the temperature of large foyers and atria, which are usually difficult to heat and cool. While the trend in green architecture is to avoid designing such large volumes, in public buildings and industrial facilities where large open spaces are required, clerestories can be a useful design solution.

During the Industrial Revolution, glass became less costly to produce, making it widely available. As buildings were fitted with larger amounts of glass, and as advancements in structural technology allowed the walls

The Crystal Palace, the largest cast iron and plate glass building when it was constructed in 1851, London, England

to be thinner and the number of columns to be reduced, natural light could penetrate more deeply into buildings. Using large amounts of glass to bring in natural light is another way to reduce the need for artificial heating and lighting, similar to clerestory windows. Passive heating and daylighting could reduce energy usage by close to 50 percent, if done correctly. To avoid incurring extra heating or cooling costs from improperly executed solutions, important design considerations include selecting windows with sufficient energy performance ratings, adding exterior shading devices, and placing the windows in a way that blocks unwanted heat from the summer sun yet captures the winter sun.

A portico, a covered space on the exterior of a building that is supported by a series of columns, is another passive technique that aids human comfort. In the Mediterranean climate of Greece, where life was once lived largely outdoors, porticos were a popular gathering place that offered protection from both the hot summer sun and the wet winters. One of the most important public buildings was the temple, where rituals were conducted; temples featured a portico on at least one side. Porticos were also often found on many other public buildings, such as markets, classrooms, courthouses, and city halls.

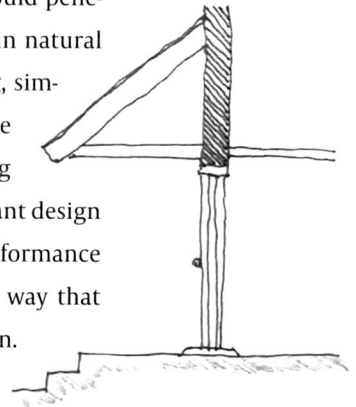

A roof overhang or exterior shade is another passive technique to block the heat of the sun from warming the interior

La Madeleine Church, including the portico was inspired by ancient Greek temples, Paris, France

Today, porticos are a way to shade a building, thus lowering the temperature inside, although they usually do not extend the entire length of a building. Porticos can also function as an overhang to provide shelter at an entrance or exit. A vestibule or small foyer similarly serves as a transitional space and, if large enough, can serve as a gathering space. From a sustainability standpoint, a foyer or a vestibule enhances the efficiency of a building's heating and cooling system by providing two sets of doors that keep out cold air during the winter months and humid air in the summer. Depending on the local climate, regional building codes may require a foyer or vestibule for certain building types.

A residential variation on the portico is the porch. The second half of the 19th century was the golden age of the porch in the United States. Besides providing a sheltered gathering place, it shaded the interior of the house from the sun. House plan books in the early 1900s published by such companies as Sears Roebuck and E. W. Stillwell & Company contained house designs that could be adapted to different climates by modifying the porch based on local sun patterns.

An arcade, a covered walkway enclosed by a succession of arches, provides similar benefits to a portico, Cloister of San Domenico, Perugia, Italy

The porch, a residential variation on the portico

Many American communities were developed using a north–south, east-west grid; therefore, if a house was not properly oriented to the path of the sun, its porch would be ineffective, eliminating any passive benefits it could provide. By the latter part of the 20th century, the porch had fallen out of fashion as a result of the proliferation of telephones, garages, backyard patios, and air conditioning.

In sustainable design today, a porch is a smart way to passively control the temperature inside a house. If positioned to block the heat of the sun in the summer, it can reduce energy usage and provide a shaded area for people to enjoy the outdoors. It can also help shield the building from snow, wind, and rain. Additionally, with a little attention to design and the particular climate of the region, porches can encourage social connections with the surrounding community.

Passive design offers many techniques for building a sustainable infrastructure of housing and public buildings that respect the environment. These techniques not only save energy over a building's life-span but also allow the mechanical systems to be downsized. The most effective results occur when passive design techniques and mechanical systems are designed in conjunction with one another. Energy is wasted if the sizing of the mechanical equipment does not account for the passive techniques being used. Several software tools are available that help architects and designers incorporate local climate data into their designs in order to maximize the cost and energy savings possible with passive design. Designing in a way that creates harmony between the passive and mechanical elements helps ensure that we use only the resources we truly need.

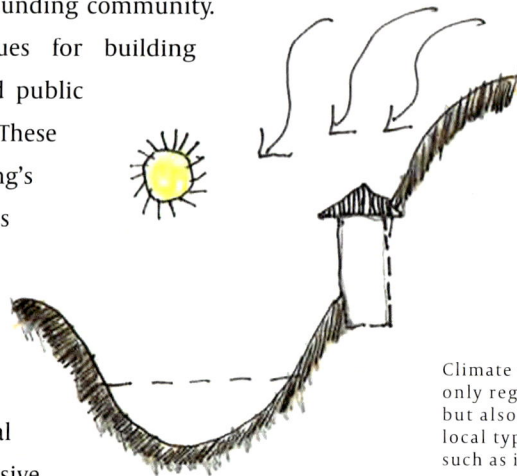

Climate varies not only regionally but also with the local typography, such as in a valley

Chapter Four:
Water Management

W ater is vital to all life on this planet, whether animal, plant, or human. To serve this basic need, organized societies have long managed water for irrigation, human consumption, hygiene, and recreation. For thousands of years, and even in the 21st century, different cultures have collected and stored water using technology that employs one or more of the same basic approaches, such as cisterns, dams, lakes, reservoirs, and canals. Transporting water has likewise remained the same, using aqueducts and pipes; now manufactured from other materials, these were once made of wood, mud-brick, or terra-cotta. Water has been harvested from various sources depending on what was available locally: wells, groundwater aquifers, natural springs, rivers, lakes, and greywater, in addition to rainfall. Humans have always faced challenges in fulfilling their need for water, including overcoming the distance it must sometimes be transported in order to reach end users, collecting and managing stormwater and

An aqueduct running through California

wastewater, ensuring water quality, and responsibly using water to avoid scarcity. Water management is as much a concern today as it has been throughout history.

The Hanging Gardens of Babylon, located near the palace of Babylon along the Euphrates River in ancient Mesopotamia, is an example of a water-management system that has practical application today. King Nebuchadnezzar II built the gardens in approximately 600 BC for Queen Sammu-ramat. The design, as represented in several ancient illustrations, featured a structure similar to the stepped design of a ziggurat temple, with stairways leading up the side. Each of the large plateaus

An ancient elevated aqueduct, Siena, Italy

The Hanging
Gardens of
Babylon

contained gardens filled with subtropical plants and flowers, which were irrigated with water from the Euphrates River. Water was pumped to the top of the structure by a screw or chain pump and channeled to the gardens on each level.

Although scholars debate whether such a place ever existed, the Hanging Gardens of Babylon illustrates a valuable water-management tool—a green roof—that offers several sustainable benefits. By capturing rainwater, which the plants gradually absorb via transpiration, a green roof keeps the water out of the stormwater system and helps prevent rivers and lakes from flooding. Germany has been designing and constructing green roofs for decades, and they are slowly gaining in popularity in the United States. Roofs constructed with shallow planting containers, which are known as extensive green roofs, grow only shallow-root plant material and are the more popular and economical type of green roof in use today. King Nebuchadnezzar's green roof garden would be considered an intensive green roof because it contained trees, which require a deeper depth of soil and a reinforced structure to support the weight of the soil and the trees. Intensive green roofs are not very economical because of the costs of modifying a structure to support the weight of the additional soil.

The ancient Greeks developed a number of water-management techniques to adapt to the area's limited water supply; Greece's only

A green roof is composed of many layers

43

rainfall occurs in winter. Besides locating their towns and cities where water was most abundant and using the steep topography of the land to transport the water by gravity, the ancient Greeks reused water as an important daily practice. Inside their homes, they used greywater—the wastewater from cooking, laundry, and bathing—for cleaning and draining the toilets. Terra-cotta pipes collected stormwater from the streets, which was used to irrigate fields.

Today, the reuse of water is considered a sustainable technique and is similar conceptually to the practices of the ancient Greeks. Wastewater collected from sinks, showers, and bathtubs can be used for flushing toilets, landscape irrigation, and other non-potable applications, although modern greywater systems for interior applications use a set of pipes separate from those for potable water. Greywater use is relatively uncommon for interior plumbing because of restrictions and limitations in building and health codes and because of the cost of installing separate pipes for potable water and greywater. On the other hand, collecting and using rainwater for irrigation is a growing practice.

Water was an important part of life in ancient Rome, and as a result, the Romans devised a number of techniques to secure an ample supply. A central component of Roman society was the public baths, where people went to socialize, exercise, and conduct business as well as to bathe and which required a significant amount of water. Many of the wealthier Roman citizens

44

The ancient Roman Baths of Caracalla, Rome, Italy

paid to have water supplied directly to their households for fountains, pools, fish-ponds, and their own private baths. As the population in ancient Rome grew, so did its need for water. Eventually the Romans had to seek out water sources beyond what was available locally from rainwater, wells, and the Tiber River. By building aqueducts they were able to transport large volumes of water over difficult terrain using gravity. The use of the arch, concrete, and advanced engineering skills made this feat possible. Eventually, 11 aqueducts served Rome, the longest of which spanned 62 miles. The Romans used aqueducts throughout their empire, and aqueducts over time became a standard method worldwide for transporting water.

An ancient Roman
aqueduct, Pont du
Gard, France

Modern aqueducts still rely on gravity to move the water, but the pipes and canals they employ are much larger than those found in ancient Roman aqueducts, and modern systems transport larger amounts of water much greater distances than Roman aqueducts. For instance, the Colorado River Aqueduct, built between 1933 and 1941, stretches 242 miles from Colorado to Los Angeles. Modern improvements to aqueducts incorporate improved water quality, facilities for storing the water, and flow controls to prevent flooding. The downside is the cost of transporting water great distances, which includes the cost of acquiring land on which to build the aqueducts as well as costs to the natural habitats that might be disturbed or displaced by their construction.

The Colorado River Aqueduct

The mouth of the Cloaca Maxima, Rome, Italy

The Romans engineered many public works projects in addition to aqueducts. The Cloaca Maxima (meaning "Greatest Sewer") was designed in the 7th century BC to drain the marshy wetlands around the Forum. Over time, bath and latrine water and stormwater flowed into the sewer, which drained directly into the Tiber River. Originally, the sewer was an open drain that lined the streets, exposing Romans to odors and disease; it was eventually enclosed to maximize street space, which controlled the smell but did not eliminate health issues.

Municipal sanitation systems to treat sewage began to be developed in the late 1800s and early 1900s. Even though modern sewers and stormwater systems function similarly to those in ancient Rome, it is preferable that sewage and stormwater systems operate separately. When a combined system overflows onto the streets during a heavy storm, raw sewage gets mixed in with the stormwater, endangering people's health. Dumping untreated waste into any body of water also creates a health hazard for humans as well as the environment. Stormwater should also be filtered to remove the chemicals (such as pesticides and motor oil), waste, debris, and dirt that frequently find their way into the system. Other current stormwater-management techniques use open space in parks, planting beds, and manmade wetlands to capture stormwater runoff naturally, which filters pollutants out, preventing them from flowing directly into natural waterways. The aging infrastructure of public sanitation systems is a pressing issue in many communities. A major challenge is the significant cost of repairing old systems, upgrading to energy-efficient technology, and integrating stormwater-management design into the landscape.

Venice's unique wetland ecosystem illustrates how nature can serve as a model for developing nonmechanical solutions, in this case for filtering and cleaning water that also promotes plant life. People first settled in Venice in the 5th century AD on a series of islands around a lagoon off the Adriatic Sea that provided transportation routes and security from barbarians. The area's salt marshes, sea grass, and changing tides helped purify the water and provided a natural habitat for plants and animals. The plants' root system filtered and absorbed pollutants,

The Grand Canal and Basilica Santa Maria della Salute, Venice, Italy

Murky water
in the lagoon,
Venice, Italy

returning clean water to the waterway. This process of natural water purification can be found wherever wetlands exist. Unfortunately, as Venice's population has increased over the last 16 centuries, the quality of the water in the lagoon and the surrounding ecosystem has degraded. Today, constructing manmade wetlands with appropriate regional plants is a water-management tool used not only to capture stormwater runoff but also to treat wastewater and sewage.

Different cultures have used various water-storage solutions, such as dams, reservoirs, and cisterns, to ensure an adequate water supply. Cisterns collect rainfall, runoff from roofs, or water transported from a distant source (like a lake or river) and store that water underground, on a rooftop, or in a garden. In ancient Crete (2600–1100 BC),

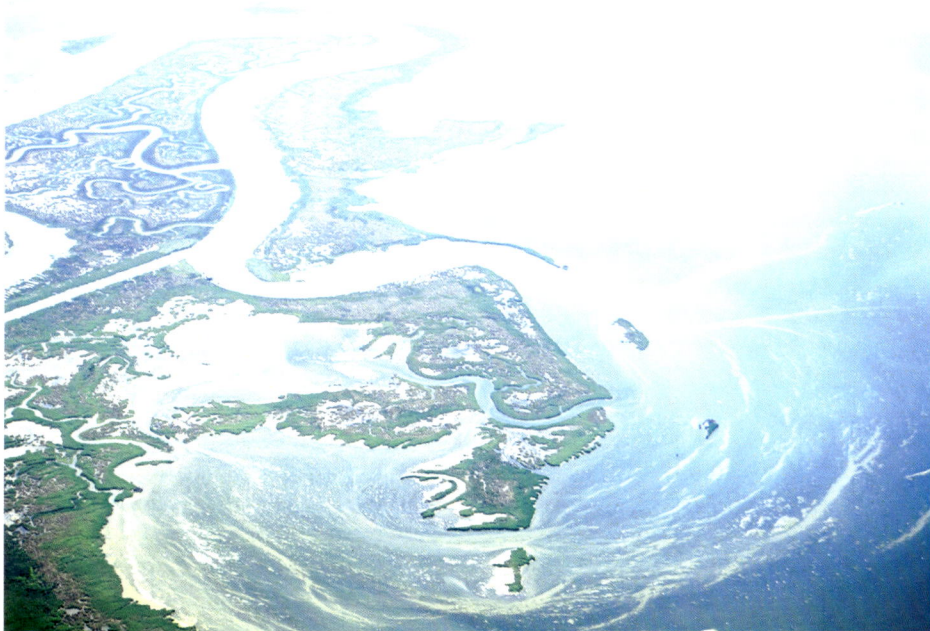

An aerial view of
the lagoon islands,
Venice Italy

A cistern under the floor of a courtyard stored rainwater, Pompeii, Italy

cisterns were used to store rainwater collected from the nearby mountains—the island's only source of water. In ancient Roman dwellings dating to 300 BC in Pompeii, cisterns placed underneath the floor of courtyards stored the rainwater that fell through the open roof. Roman apartment buildings had open-roofed courtyards and cisterns as well. One of history's largest and most impressive underground cisterns is the Basilica Cistern in Constantinople (now Istanbul), completed in AD 532 to supply water to the Great Palace and surrounding buildings. It stored 2.8 million cubic feet of water, which was delivered by aqueduct from a forest 12 miles to the north.

The current focus on water conservation has revived interest in cisterns and other water-storage techniques like reservoirs and rain barrels. In regions of the world facing major droughts, rainwater storage is critical for supplying people's daily water needs. Using reservoirs to store rainwater is more feasible for supplying water to communities with large populations because they have more capacity than cisterns, although the construction of large reservoirs can displace communities and damage ecosystems. Small-scale reservoirs could have fewer repercussions

The
Basilica
Cistern,
Istanbul,
Turkey

but need to be supplemented by another water source because of the amount of evaporation that occurs. A natural lake can supply water to a community without the negative impacts of a large reservoir. A variety of storage strategies is necessary in order to adequately address varying rainfall levels across the globe and changes in rainfall as a result of climate change. Areas with higher levels of annual rainfall, for instance, require different solutions than areas prone to drought.

Horsetooth Reservoir, Fort Collins, Colorado

The pre-Columbian Hohokam culture (AD 200–1450), located in what is now southern Arizona, also practiced water management. Open irrigation canals connected to the Gila, Salt, and Santa Cruz Rivers were built to water the corn crops, while

Open irrigation canals in a corn field

52

domestic water came from wells. Each community was built around a single canal or series of canals, and each community took ownership of the land surrounding its canals. The construction and operation of the canals was labor intensive, which united the people and gave each family the right to use the water. Maintenance of the canals, including opening and closing the gates to regulate the flow of water, became a group responsibility and ensured that the crops had adequate water to grow.

Modern governments are responsible for providing their citizens with clean drinking water and building and maintaining sanitation services. When upgrading public services, governments should consider the lessons that can be learned from the technical strength of the Roman Empire's water infrastructure and the communal strength of the Hohokam culture. Public water systems must be designed

Native American cliff dwellings, Flagstaff, Arizona

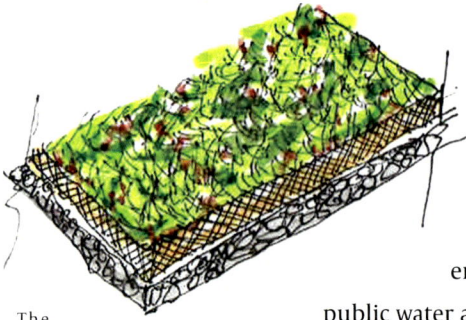

The different layers of a green roof

and maintained with an emphasis on efficiency and on implementing green solutions—like parks, open space, and green roofs—that not only give people enjoyment but also benefit the community's public water and sanitation systems. Wetlands and other eco-friendly ways of filtering stormwater can reduce the size and cost of water-treatment plants. Using natural flood plains to collect water for consumption is a better alternative to building dams or levees. Building green infrastructure requires collaboration among governments, academia, nongovernmental organizations, and the private sector and needs support from the communities themselves. When designing sustainable water infrastructure, the differing social structures, economic resources, and climatic conditions of each community must be considered as well.

If we want to achieve what the United Nations (UN) Conference on Environment and Development has called for—that every generation should have the same access to equality, development, and the environment—providing clean water for all is a problem that still requires solutions. Two of the biggest water challenges addressed in the annual UN World Water Development Report are ensuring that all people can meet their water needs, particularly as the world's population increases, and empowering communities to take steps to protect their water resources. The International Water Association believes that proper and equitable management of water resources creates a sustainable environment for humans. Water is crucial to the survival of humans as well as to plant and animal life; it should not be considered a commodity for the economic benefit of those supplying it.

54

Chapter Five:
Green Legislation

D uring the course of written history, laws have been used to regulate different aspects of the built environment in order to protect building occupants and the larger community as well as the natural world. Providing access to clean drinking water and sunlight, ensuring that builders construct safe structures, and using energy-efficient materials are just some of the ways laws have been used to govern building practices. In the late 20th century—when information became more readily available and shared—a global awareness spread about the large-scale harm humans, including buildings, have had on the environment since the Industrial Revolution. Building-related laws are particularly important now, amid increasing pressure on the environment from the world's expanding population and building construction. Laws such as building codes and zoning ordinances can be used to ensure that sustainable techniques are integrated into new and renovated buildings.

Building-related laws are integral to protecting the environment, Los Angeles, California

The idea of using building codes to protect people and communities from injury and destruction resulting from faulty design or workmanship or a catastrophic event is believed to have originated in ancient Babylon.

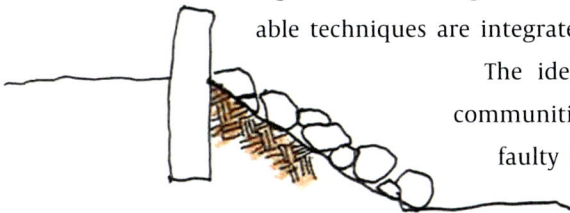

A retaining wall prevents soil erosion

During his reign (1792–1750 BC), King Hammurabi enacted the Code of Hammurabi, which contained 282 laws governing the Babylonian people. Among them was a law that called for the death of the builder of any structure that collapsed in which a person died. In 1221, London passed a mandate prohibiting thatched roofs because of their flammability and the potential for a roof fire to spread easily throughout the city. Allowable materials included wooden shingles (usually oak),

58

stone slabs (usually slate, which could be cut thin), and clay tiles. In the United States, building codes were enacted as far as back as the 1600s to address fire safety.

Current building codes in the United States, which include many more requirements in addition to fire safety, have been in existence since the early 1900. They provide a road map for the design and construction of buildings to protect the safety, health, and welfare of their occupants, safeguarding them from fire, structural failures, and general hazards. Beginning in 1975, as a result of rising oil prices, building codes started to address environmental issues related to the amount of energy buildings consume, adding energy-conserving requirements that apply to insulation and the window-to-wall ratio (the amount of glass in an exterior wall).

Terra-cotta roof tiles offer durability and fireproofing, Bavaria, Germany

Zoning ordinances, another type of building-related law in use today, regulate how a property can be used. Some neighborhoods restrict commercial buildings by allowing only single-family homes to be built, for example, while others restrict the density by limiting the height of buildings. Building-height limitations also protect people's access to light by requiring that the square footage of higher floors decrease as the building rises, which allows a greater amount of sunlight to reach the street level.

Laws written for similar purposes can be found in the ancient world. The Romans believed that exposure to the sun was essential to people's health and well-being and that everyone, whether Roman citizen or not, should have access to sunlight for drying clothes and

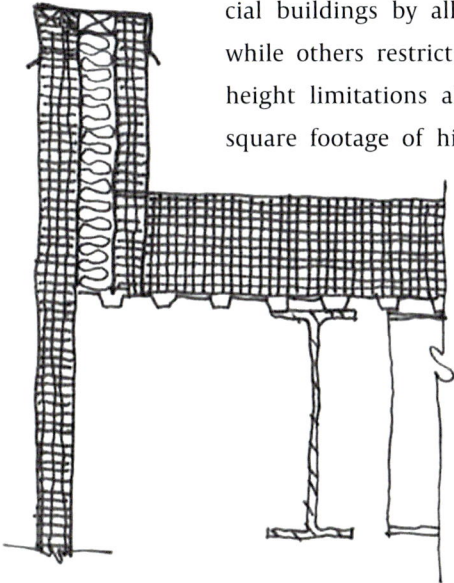

Insulation reduces the amount of energy buildings consume

59

Zoning ordinances often require tall
buildings to be set back as they rise to allow
sunlight to reach the street, Chicago, Illinois

growing food. During the rule of Emperor Justinian I (AD 527–565), Roman civil laws, called servitudes (personal rights), allowed building owners to make openings in a neighbor's property if it blocked sunlight from reaching their buildings. Currently, several US states have solar rights laws or local zoning ordinances that give a property or the solar panels on a building the right to unrestricted sunlight.

Past cultures have used conservation laws to protect waterways, land development, and animals. The water supply in ancient Rome was tainted with dirt from the streets and waste from latrines. In AD 80, the Roman Senate passed laws to protect the city's supply of potable water for bathing and drinking. During the 14th century,

The polluted
Tiber River,
Rome, Italy

the English Parliament outlawed the practice of dumping waste in waterways to keep the potable water clean. In America during the Colonial period, William Penn wrote Pennsylvania's first conservation law, in 1681, which required that one acre of trees be preserved for every five acres of land cleared.

Four decades later, in 1721, Pennsylvania governor Sir William Keith enacted a law that protected deer in that state from being hunted between January and July. Benjamin Franklin petitioned in 1739 to prevent tanneries from dumping their manufacturing waste into the Delaware River; he later led a commission that regulated water-pollution levels.

William Penn,
a conservationist

The conservation movement as we know it today began in North America in the late 1800s. It came about as a response to the destruction of virgin forests by logging, the ill effects of contemporary agriculture, and the alarming extinction rate of animals. The formation of the movement was aided by a growing awareness of the human relationship to plants, animals, and weather conditions that emerged from the birth of modern geography in the mid-1800s. In the early 1900s, President Theodore Roosevelt initiated some of the earliest conservation laws to protect the nation's water and animal life from human intervention. This conservation mindset extended to the built environment during the 20th century, when laws were passed to preserve older

Benjamin Franklin,
an environmentalist

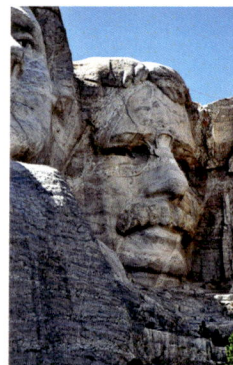

Theodore Roosevelt, a protector of water

buildings that are significant from an architectural, historical, or cultural perspective. Although the preservation of buildings is not usually considered a sustainable technique, it complements the goals of the sustainability movement. Preserving a variety of structures around the world helps us see how past cultures created solutions that used local material and passive design techniques. Reusing and renovating buildings, rather than building new structures, also conserves natural resources and reduces the amount of waste added to landfills.

Properly managing timber
forests prevents them from
being depleted

Preserving buildings complements the goals of the sustainability movement, Paris, France

Traditional adobe and tile roof construction was common in the southwestern United States prior to the 20th century

During the 20th century, the consumption of natural resources grew, human population levels rose, and air and water pollution increased. The Industrial Revolution brought many technological advances to the building industry, but it also made it possible to design buildings in a way that prioritizes human desires over other considerations—particularly the environment. The carbon footprint of buildings has increased over the last 150 years due to the increase in the square footage of buildings, the use of mechanical heating, cooling and ventilation systems powered by fossil fuels, and the invention of new building materials that require a large amount of energy to manufacture.

Amid the growing affluence in the West, scientists, conservationists, and writers began to raise public awareness about the need to protect the environment. Publications like Rachel Carson's *Silent Spring* (published in 1962) educated the public about the fragility and indispensability of the natural environment and the harm humans have caused it. The US Environmental

The EPA Headquarters, Washington, DC

Protection Agency—founded in 1970 to protect people and the environment from the ill effects of human activity—has been instrumental in the passage of many laws to ensure clean water and air and to protect wildlife. In 1987, the World Commission on Environment and Development convened to promote the need for sustainable development. The commission adopted a definition of sustainability that has since been widely cited around the globe: "Sustainable development is development that meets the needs of the present without compromising the ability of future generations to meet their own needs." The commission helped galvanize the sustainable architecture movement. Since 2000, the architecture profession has become increasingly focused on sustainability, including protecting land, reducing

Wind turbines provide cleaner energy
than oil-based forms, Wyoming prairie

our dependency on nonrenewable energy sources, conserving water, lessening the impact of building materials on the environment, and increasing air quality inside buildings. As a result, publications, building codes, government incentives, private initiatives, and marketing tools have been created to promote sustainable design and construction.

One of the initiatives that has fueled the building industry's awareness and adoption of sustainable practices is the Leadership in Energy and Environmental Design (LEED) program. This voluntary green-building rating system, launched in 1998 by the US Green Building Council, provides a series of measurements for the design, construction, operation, and maintenance of buildings that encourages the use of more sustainable solutions. It uses a point system: the more sustainable attributes a project has, the higher the level of certification it will achieve—an affirmation of the building's integration of ecologically beneficial components and cost-saving energy efficiencies.

Rainwater storage

Rating and certification systems like LEED and Green Globes (which was established in 2004 and is administered by the Green Building Initiative) have helped to educate design and construction professionals about best practices and to promote the need for sustainable buildings among building owners and the general public, but they are limited in the change they can effect. These programs are largely voluntary, especially in the private sector, and not all building owners are willing to spend the extra money to have their buildings certified. Therefore, municipalities need to adopt green building codes to ensure that all local projects address issues of sustainability. Whereas building codes are written to protect buildings and their occupants from external forces, such as earthquakes, floods, or fire, green building codes protect

Taipei 101
received LEED
platinum
certification
in 2011,
Taipei, Taiwan

the environment from the construction and operation of buildings. Green building codes can enforce such sustainable approaches as building with local materials, using passive design techniques, and incorporating water-conservation methods.

In 2012 the International Code Council released the International Green Construction Code (IgCC), a green building code that has since been adopted by a handful of states in the United States. Widespread implementation of green building codes would raise the standards for all elements of building design and construction in several areas, such as energy and water efficiency, a building's impact on the land, the disposal of construction waste, what building materials are used, and the quality and comfort of the interior environment. For example, the IgCC addresses light pollution to control unwanted glare and light trespass at night, which increases

Light pollution in the city of Bogota, Colombia

access to the nighttime sky. Healthy sound levels inside buildings are also indicated in the code to mitigate the illness and decreased productivity that occurs from noise pollution.

Another way building codes can be used is to mandate the incorporation of survivability techniques into the design of buildings to maintain critical life-supporting conditions in the event of extreme weather or other catastrophic events. Passive survivability principles require that a building is designed in such a way that it

Green building codes can be used to control light pollution, an unobstructed view of the Milky Way

can maintain livable conditions, such as keeping the temperature regulated and the air well-ventilated when access to the power grid and water supply is disabled. Passive design techniques are invaluable in providing a safe, habitable environment in such situations. For example, integrating on-site renewable energy will power essential mechanical systems. Requiring on-site water storage will allow basic plumbing services to function. Proper insulation will help maintain a consistent and comfortable temperature inside, while operable windows will provide natural light and ventilation.

Buildings can be designed to naturally release into the cool night sky the warm air that builds up inside during the day

71

Building codes exist to enforce safety in extreme situations, although they have yet to address passive survivability. Interest in passive survivability is growing, however. In the aftermath of Hurricane Katrina, design and building professionals drafted the New Orleans Principles, a set of 10 guidelines that address how sustainability should be managed in the post-Katrina reconstruction of the city. One of the principles calls for new and rebuilt buildings to incorporate passive survivability techniques. Some professionals see the need for passive survivability beyond disaster preparedness to make sure that our building infrastructure is functional during power outages, fuel or water shortages, and changes in local weather patterns caused by climate change.

Our buildings need to incorporate innovative thinking. Sustainable design should provide occupants with a safe and healthy environment that limits the building's ecological footprint and facilitates the responsible stewardship of the planet's natural resources. The legal system—through standard building codes and green building codes, zoning ordinances, and other planning tools—can ensure that architects, engineers, contractors, building product manufacturers, and building owners use best practices when designing, constructing, and operating buildings.

Conservation laws protect our coastlines, Oregon

Chapter Six:
Writings on Architecture

Architects, builders, engineers, and theoreticians throughout history have written books about architecture that provide instructions for designing and constructing buildings and present different theories about design. Some of these writings are valuable for architects in the 21st century, offering design concepts, techniques, and directions regarding how to build in a way that is sustainable. These sources also contain useful ideas about how nature can supplement architecture, such as how the sun shining through a building not only provides beautiful illumination but can keep occupants healthy. Many of the sustainable approaches employed today—such as using durable materials, creating a relationship between a building and the local climate, and conserving water resources—can be found in historic writings based on Greek and Roman architectural practices and thought.

The Hanging Gardens of Babylon

Marcus Vitruvius Pollio, born between 80 and 70 BC, was a Roman architect and engineer. He wrote the multivolume *De Architectura* (published in English as *Ten Books on Architecture*), the first acclaimed handbook on engineering and architecture. It provided practical information about building roads, heating water

Sustainability is about creating a relationship between a building and the local climate, Madagascar, Africa

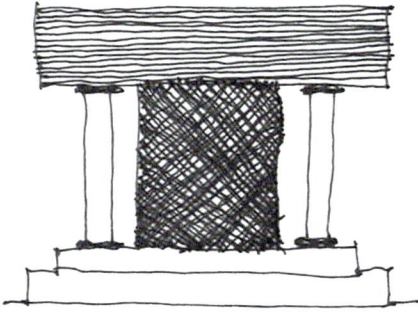

A typical overhang on a Greek Temple

for public baths, using proportions to create visual beauty, creating a healthy environment for building occupants, and storing and using raw materials—all based on the principle of connecting humans and nature. Vitruvius used the symmetry of the human body as a fundamental proportion system when designing temples, colonnades, rooms, and doors. He was a strong believer in the architectural conventions developed by the Greeks, which he believed should be the foundation of all design. Copies of the book survived in manuscript form; when it was printed during the Renaissance, Vitruvius's ideas spread, becoming a strong influence on Western architecture.

Vitruvius espoused six fundamental principles for the design of buildings, some of which are viable sustainable design techniques for modern buildings. For instance, he instructed that spaces needing consistent light with little glare should face north. Current daylighting guidelines also advise using the north side of a building for rooms that need steady, cool, indirect light—such as galleries or artist studios—and suggest exterior or internal shading to control glare on the south, east, and west facades. In his street designs, Vitruvius used wind maps to determine the placement of walls in order to shield pedestrians from the wind. Today, windbreak design using wind maps is a contemporary sustainable strategy that

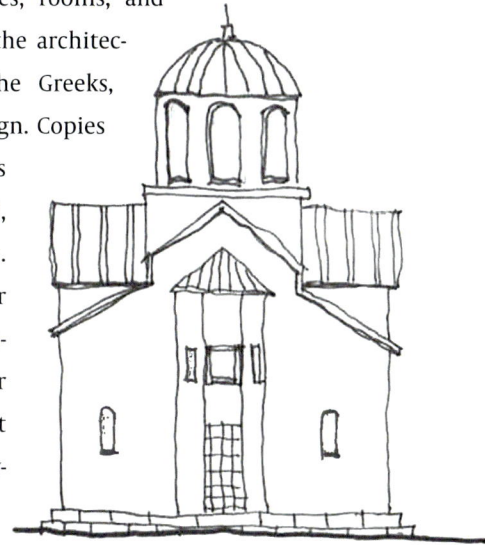

The clerestory window underneath the dome naturally illuminates the interior

An ancient Roman temple, Lebanon

77

employs a combination of trees, buildings, and walls to reduce wind velocity and create a comfortable environment protected from undesirable winter winds.

Among those influenced by Vitruvius were the Italian Renaissance architects Leon Battista Alberti and Andrea Palladio; their buildings can still be found in Italy. Alberti's *De Re Aedificatoria* (*On the Art of Building*), published in 1452, contains 10 sections, each devoted to a particular topic. The book's primary purpose was to serve as a guide for managing the relationship between natural resources

A row of trees acts as a wind break, Denmark

78

and the built environment. For instance, the public works section explains how to design a bridge to preserve the river banks. Alberti advised studying the river's currents when designing the shape of the piers. He also counseled that the ideal site for a bridge is one where the natural landforms are not too steep so the land does not have to be disturbed. The section on the work of individuals recommends determining the layout of rooms using the angle of the sun and the wind patterns at different times of the year to optimize comfort.

Among sustainable techniques in use today is the passive design approach of siting a building in such a way as to harness the sun and wind to help control the interior temperature, reducing dependence on both mechanical systems and the fossil fuels used to power them. Recent studies have shown that natural light offers many health and performance benefits to a building's occupants: exposure to daylight increases productivity and helps the

A bridge constructed in harmony with the landform

Palladio (*above*) believed that both the functional and the aesthetic are what define a building

79

body regulate circadian rhythms. In addition, properly placed and sized windows provide views to the outdoors, creating spaces that are pleasant to be in and portals through which people can connect with the natural world.

Palladio, an architect who trained as a stonemason and sculptor, wrote *I Quattro Libri dell'Architettura* (*The Four Books of Architecture*). Published in 1570, it was translated into every major European language. The widespread popularity of the book created a language of architecture called Palladianism, whose vocabulary was derived from Palladio's designs and which influenced architecture in Europe and North America into the 18th century. For instance, the three-part window containing a large arched center window flanked by two narrower rectilinear ones is known as a Palladian window. In contrast to Vitruvius, who was influenced by Greek architecture, Palladio based his designs on Roman architecture.

A clerestory in an Egyptian temple

The majority of Palladio's book promoted the idea that a design solution to a problem must be not only functional but also visually beautiful. For instance, a roof should both have an aesthetically pleasing appearance and account for the local climate, particularly the amount of rain and snow it receives. Palladio's design for the Villa Capra in Vicenza demonstrates this approach. The sloping roof is capped with a central dome topped with a cupola containing a band of windows, allowing light into the interior. The angle of the roof sheds water, preventing the roof from rotting from standing rainwater, and the dome adds an element of visual delight both inside and out. Symmetry was important to Palladio

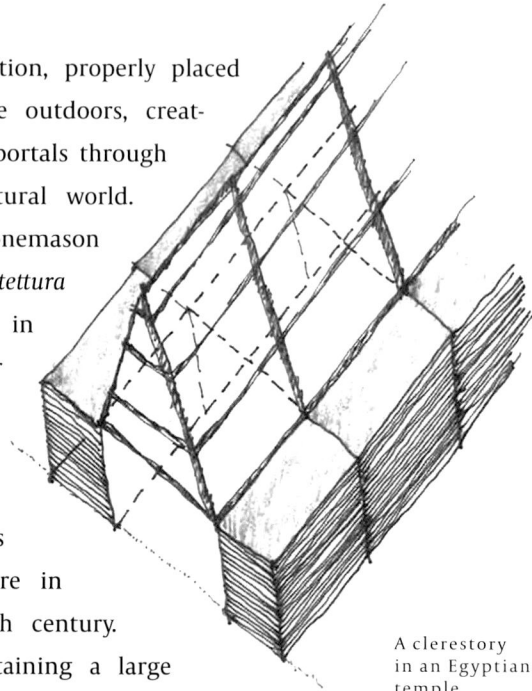

80

Right: Palladian window, Christ Church, Philadelphia, Pennsylvania

Wind energy combines the tangible (the windy landscape) with the intangible (the energy potential of the wind)

Left:
Villa Capra, designed by Palladio, Vicenza, Italy

as well; each of the four sides of the square structure contains a portico topped by a sloping roof, which shields the interior from the hot southern Italian summer sun while adding a sense of grandeur to all four facades. He believed that function and visual beauty are intertwined. Creating something that is both beautiful and functional is what connects the art and the science of architecture. Palladio's writings and designs teach us that sustainable architecture can appeal to our senses—although, unfortunately, some people today think that designing in a sustainable manner cannot produce beautiful results.

Amid these and other historical writings are hints of sustainable design techniques and ideologies, including the obligation that humans must care for the environment. Christian Norberg-Schulz, a 20th-century Norwegian architect, architectural historian, and theorist, is one contemporary writer who is continuing the legacy of past architectural theorists. He has written several books about architecture's role in connecting humans to nature. Norberg-Schulz sees our connection to nature as having both tangible and intangible components that occur every day and are unique to different climates and cultures. The tangible aspects of nature are the different types of landscapes, such as mountains, valleys, and low country; the intangible are the things we have no control over, such as the course of the sun throughout the year and the amount of cloud cover on any given day. These everyday tangible and intangible phenomena create a unique sense of place through which humans and architecture can coexist with nature. Norberg-Schulz's solution for reducing the impact of the built world on the environment is to design cities and buildings using his concept of place—to unite the tangible and intangible through design. One example is to harness the intangible renewable energy from the sun or wind, as is feasible given the tangible features of a landscape in a particular region, in order to lower the use of fossil fuels and to embrace the landscape, rather than destroy it.

Left and above:
The built environment can
successfully coexist with nature,
Saarburg, Germany

85

Theory is an important subject in the teaching of architecture, along with history. Architectural theory and history reveal to us a metaphysical connection between science and nature, a connection to past societies, and knowledge about how ancient cultures coexisted with the seasons and the landscape. Much of the architecture built during the 20th century was designed for the betterment of humans without concern for the natural environment. We need writers like Norberg-Schulz, Vitruvius, Palladio, Alberti, and many others to teach us how to design and construct buildings with respect and care for the environment and how to create beautiful and comfortable spaces in which to live and work.

Santa Maria
Novella by Alberti,
Florence, Italy

Chapter Seven:
The Beauty of Sustainability

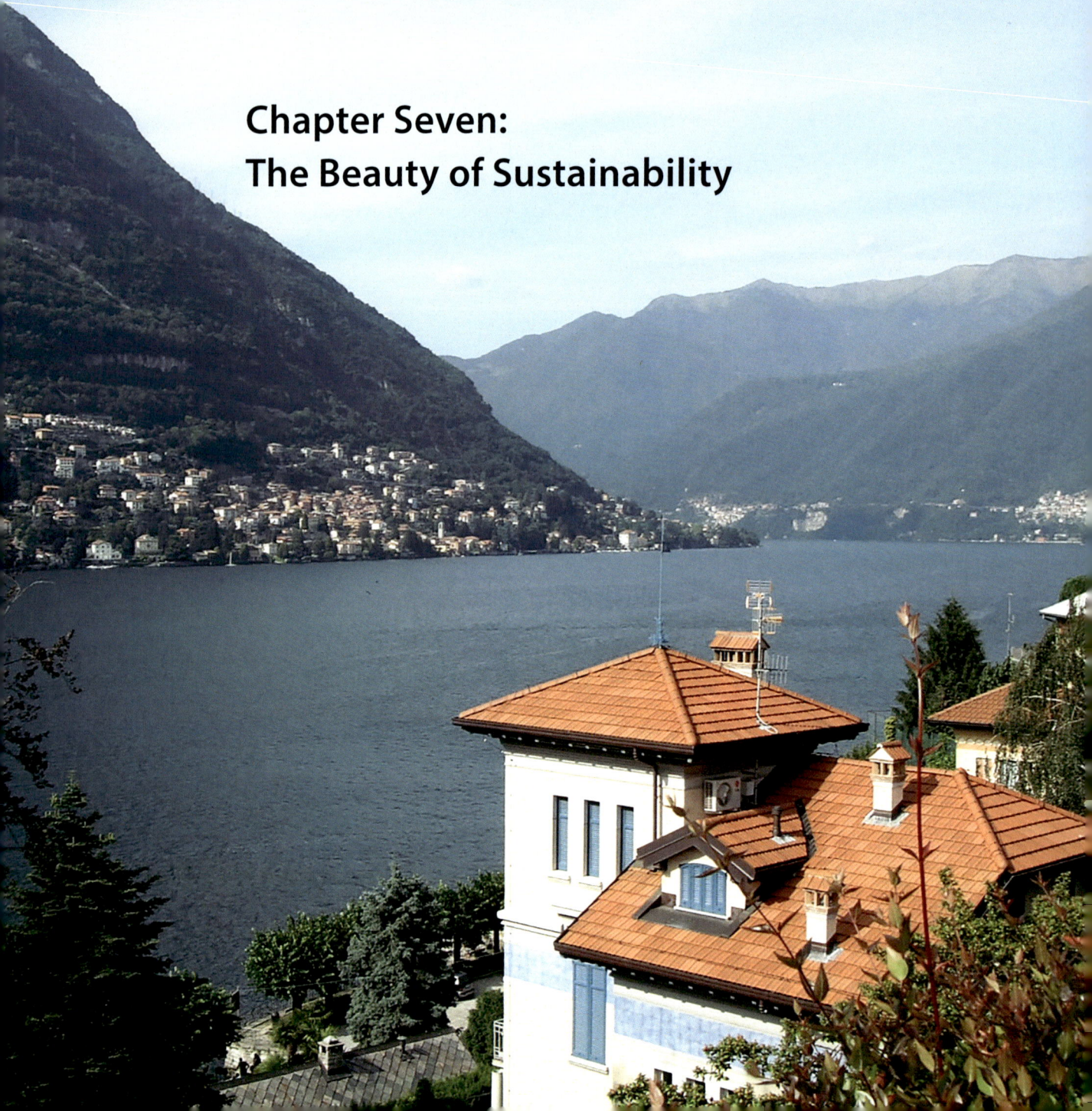

As an art, architecture offers an aesthetic beauty based on proportions and an understanding of the synthesis of forms. This visible beauty is seen in a building's form and shape, the color and texture of its walls, the ornamentation, and the arrangement of its spaces. G. R. H. Wright, in volume 1 of *Ancient Building Technology*, states that technology is "not directly linked to aesthetics—it cannot be judged according to the artistic worth of its product." I see it differently. I think there is a link between technology and the beauty of architecture. A building's sustainable technology produces an intellectual beauty that complements its aesthetic beauty. Intellectual beauty may not always be visible to the human eye, much as the inner functioning of our body is invisible to us. A building's intellectual beauty can be found inside its walls and under its roof, in such things as how efficient building components can provide a comfortable environment for the occupants while lowering the amount of energy needed to operate the building.

Comfortable temperatures, low noise levels, and good air quality are all part of the intellectual beauty of a building that enhances human well-being in the 21st century world of

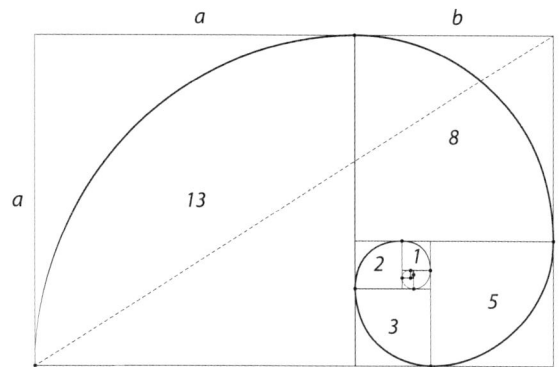

The golden ratio has been used in architecture since antiquity to create a sense of beauty through harmony and proportion

Roof dormers not only break up the mass of a roof but also aid natural ventilation

Wind
turbines,
Yorkshire,
England

The largest brick dome every built, Santa Marie del Fiore Cathedral, Florence, Italy

sustainability. Technical building components that are sustainable include water-saving fixtures, high-performance heating and cooling systems, energy-saving appliances and lighting fixtures, wind turbines, and solar panels. Even though many of these are utilitarian, they are nonetheless beautiful in the responsive way they provide solutions that reduce a building's consumption of natural resources. Durable and locally manufactured materials, passive design elements, and water-conservation practices are all poetic in their respect for the planet.

The Egyptian pyramids are beautiful not only for their form but also for the construction techniques that have enabled the buildings to stand for 4,500 years

Sustainability is about balancing visual beauty and intellectual beauty. To think that architecture is solely concerned with visible beauty is to miss the benefits that users, the surrounding community, and the planet gain from a building's intellectual beauty. True beauty occurs when all the elements that make up the whole—both visible and invisible—are in harmony. There is beauty both in how something looks and in how it works.

For thousands of years, architects and non-architects alike have designed buildings using simple technologies and local materials, providing us with much knowledge and wisdom about sustainable design. There is beauty in that simple weep hole used in the Giza pyramids in Egypt that have kept their walls from deteriorating. The Greeks designed beautiful gutters that shed water from their buildings, helping to preserve many notable structures for our study and enjoyment. The Romans taught us about the durability of concrete, and the Chinese showed us that wood from old buildings can be reused in new ones. Porches, courtyards, and clerestory windows have been incorporated into the buildings of many cultures as creative and functional architectural elements.

A building has a form, fulfills a function for its occupants, and carries a responsibility to fit into the surrounding ecosystem—and it can be beautiful at the same time. To separate the aesthetics of architecture and the technology of sustainability is like separating the breath from the body. Creating architecture that is both intellectual and beautiful can be one of man's greatest gifts to the planet Earth.

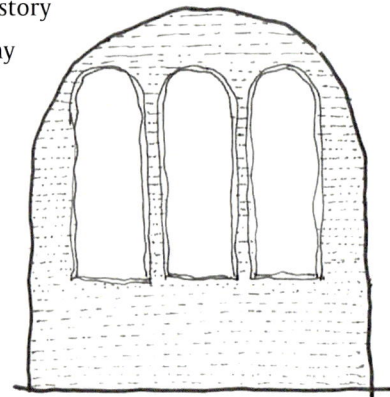

Windows connect building occupants to nature

Alberti, Leon Battista. *On the Art of Building in Ten Books.* Translated by Joseph Rykwert, Neil Leach, and Robert Tavernor. Cambridge, MA: MIT Press, 1988.

Alexander, Christopher, Sara Ishikawa, and Murray Silverstein. *A Pattern Language: Towns, Buildings, Construction.* New York: Oxford University Press, 1977.

Attmann, Osman. *Green Architecture: Advanced Technologies and Materials.* New York: McGraw-Hill, 2010.

Banham, Reyner. *The Architecture of the Well-Tempered Environment.* 2nd ed. Chicago: University of Chicago Press, 1984.

Brand, Stewart. *How Buildings Learn: What Happens after They're Built.* New York: Penguin Books, 1994.

Boris, Franco. *Leon Battista Alberti: The Complete Works.* New York: Harper & Row, 1975.

Chadwick, Robert. *First Civilizations: Ancient Mesopotamia and Ancient Egypt.* Oakville, CT: Equinox, 2005.

Coldstream, Nicola. *Medieval Architecture.* New York: Oxford University Press, 2002.

Coulton, J. J. *Ancient Greek Architects at Work: Problems of Structure and Design.* Ithaca, NY: Cornell University Press, 1977.

Crouch, Dora P. *Water Management in Ancient Greek Cities.* New York: Oxford University Press, 1993.

Dalley, Stephanie. *The Mystery of the Hanging Garden of Babylon: An Elusive World Wonder Traced.* Oxford: Oxford University Press, 2013.

Dolan, Michael. *The American Porch: An Informal History of an Informal Place*. Guilford, CT: Lyons, 2002.

Donnelly, Marian C. *Architecture in Colonial America*. Edited by Leland M. Roth. Eugene: University of Oregon Press, 2003.

Donough, William, and Michael Braungart. *Cradle to Cradle: Remaking the Way We Make Things*. New York: North Point, 2002.

Earth Pledge Foundation, comp. *Sustainable Architecture: White Papers*. New York: Earth Pledge Foundation, 2000.

Fish, Suzanne K., and Paul R. Fish, eds. *The Hohokam Millennium*. Santa Fe, NM: School for Advanced Research Press, 2008.

Hobday, Richard. *The Light Revolution: Health, Architecture and the Sun*. Forres, Scotland: Findhorn, 2006.

Hitchcock, Henry-Russell, Albert Fein, Winston Weisman, and Vincent Scully. *The Rise of an American Architecture*. Edited by Edgar Kaufmann Jr. New York: Praeger / Metropolitan Museum of Art, 1970.

Juuti, Petri, Tapio S. Katko, and Heikki S. Vuorinen. *Environmental History of Water: Global Views on Community Water Supply and Sanitation*. London: IWA, 2007.

Lowry, Bates. *Renaissance Architecture*. New York: George Braziller, 1979.

Lotz, Wolfgang. *Studies in Italian Renaissance Architecture*. Cambridge, MA: MIT Press, 1977.

Norberg-Schulz, Christian. *Genius Loci: Towards a Phenomenology of Architecture*. New York: Rizzoli, 1980.

Norberg-Schulz, Christian. *Meaning in Western Architecture*. New York: Rizzoli, 1980.

Ousterhout, Robert G. *Master Builders of Byzantium*. Philadelphia: University of Pennsylvania Museum of Archaeology and Anthropology, 2008.

Palladio, Andrea, and Adolf K. Placzek. *The Four Books of Architecture*. New York: Dover, 1965.

Pollio, Marcus Vitruvious. *Vitruvius: The Ten Books on Architecture*. Translated by Morris Hicky Morgan. Cambridge, MA: Harvard University Press, 2004.

Portoghesi, Paolo, and Vincent Scully. *After Modern Architecture*. New York: Rizzoli, 1980.

Rael, Ronald. *Earth Architecture*. New York: Princeton Architectural Press, 2009.

Raskin, Eugene. *Architecturally Speaking*. New York: Bloch, 1966.

Rosenau, Helen, and Etienne Louis Boullée. *Boullée and Visionary Architecture*. London: Academy Editions, 1976.

Stalley, Roger A. *Early Medieval Architecture*. New York: Oxford University Press, 1999.

Tavernor, Robert. *On Alberti and the Art of Building*. New Haven, CT: Yale University Press, 1998.

Wheeler, Mortimer. *Roman Art and Architecture*. The World of Art. New York: Oxford University Press, 1964.

Yanxin, Cai. *Chinese Architecture*. Cambridge, UK: Cambridge University Press, 2011.

Yegül, Fikret K. *Bathing in the Roman World*. New York: Cambridge University Press, 2010.

Young, David E., and Michiko Young. *The Art of Japanese Architecture*. North Clarendon, VT: Tuttle, 2007.

Photo Credits

Index

Note: Page numbers in italics refer to images.

A

adobe bricks. *See* mud-bricks

Adriatic Sea, 48

air conditioning. *See* heating and cooling

air pollution, 9, 66

alabaster, 16

Alahambra (Grenada, Spain), 11

Alberti, Leon Battista, 78–79, 86

Ancient Building Technology (G. R. H. Wright), 89

ancient Greece
    architecture and building, 13, 36, 77, 92
    city planning, 32
    environmental damage, 5
    water management, 43–44, 49–50

ancient Mesopotamia, 42

ancient Rome. *See also* aqueducts; Baths of Caracalla (Rome, Italy); Coliseum; Forum; Pantheon; public baths
    architecture and building, 34, 47, 50, 75, 92
    civil laws (servitudes), 59, 61
    concrete construction, 17–18
    environmental damage, 5

aqueducts
    modern, *41,* 46, *46*
    Roman, 12, *12,* 18, *42, 45,* 45–46

aquifers, 41

arcades, *37*

arches, 18

architectural beauty, 80, 83, 89

architectural history, 5, 28–29, 75, 77–80, 83, 86, 92

architectural theory, 86

atria, 35

B

Babylon, 57–58, *58*

bamboo, 15–16, *16*

basalt, 16

Basilica Cistern (Constantinople/Istanbul), 51, *51*

Basilica Santa Maria della Salute (Venice, Italy), *48*

Baths of Caracalla (Rome, Italy), 18, *44*

beauty, intellectual, 89, 92

beauty, visual, 80, 83, 89, 92

bricks, kiln-dried, 9, 11–13, 21. *See also* mud-bricks

bridges, 19, 79, *79*

building codes, 57–59, 68, 71–72

building codes, green, 68, 70–72

building materials, 9–10, *10,* 20–22, 58–59. *See also* bamboo; bricks, kiln-dried; cast iron; concrete; glass; metal; mud-bricks; palm branches; reeds; steel; stone; terra-cotta; wood

buildings. *See also* cathedrals; dwellings and homes; public baths; skyscrapers and tall buildings
    demolition of, 3
    energy use by, 3, 25–26, 28, 59, 91
    intellectual beauty of, 89
    life-span of, 17
    orientation of, *5,* 32, 35, 37–38, 77, 79
    preservation of, 62–63, *64*–65
    water use by, 3

by-products, use of, 10, 18, 22

C

canals, 52–53

carbon dioxide, 9. *See also* climate change

Suzanne Sowinski, AIA, LEED AP, GGP, ENV SP, is the president and director of sustainable building at Sowinski Sullivan Architects, a 50-person architecture and engineering firm that specializes in transportation and infrastructure projects across North America. The firm prides itself on its design process, which utilizes many of the resilient and sustainable building techniques illustrated in this book. Sowinski is an alumna of the New York Institute of Technology architecture program and the Boston Architectural College sustainable design program, where she also created the graduate course Learning From Sustainable Design through History. A registered architect in multiple states, she has been practicing architecture for over 30 years and has an MBA in sustainable business.